Pat and Margaret

VICTORIA WOOD *Pat and Margaret*

Methuen

Grateful thanks are due to the actors who appear
in photographs on the following pages:

Melissa Allen (p. 9), Jan Alphonse (pp. 9, 11, 13, 16),
Roger Brierley (p. 35), Frances Cox (p. 58),
Jeillo Edwards (p. 32), Deborah Grant (pp. 14, 23, 43,
49, 79, 88–90), Joane Hall (pp. 17, 62), Don Henderson
(pp. 43, 49, 79, 88, 90), Julie Hesmondhalgh (p. 17),
Madge Hindle (p. 73), Thora Hird (pp. 15, 46, 48, 51–2,
66, 69, 70, 74, 92–3), Celia Imrie (pp. 14, 24, 29,
31–3, 36, 43–4, 58–60, 66, 69, 79, 82), Robert Kingswell
(pp. 2, 81–2), Peter Lorenzelli (p. 49), Philip Lowrie
(pp. 16, 19), Charles Pemberton (p. 57), Amanda Pointer
(pp. 18, 19, 33–4), Duncan Preston (pp. 8, 9, 46, 48, 51,
57, 59, 60, 66, 77–9, 92–3), Anne Reid (pp. 18, 21, 24,
26, 33–4), Lynda Rooke (pp. 9, 11, 13, 16, 19, 22, 48),
Sammy-Jo Smith (p. 9), Shirley Stelfox (pp. 83–7, 90, 95),
Gemma Wardle (pp. 71–2) and Julie Walters (throughout)

First published in Great Britain 1994
by Methuen London
an imprint of Reed Consumer Books Ltd
Michelin House, 81 Fulham Road, London SW3 6RB
and Auckland, Melbourne, Singapore and Toronto

Reprinted 1994

Copyright © 1994 by Victoria Wood
The author has asserted her moral rights

Stills photographs copyright © 1994 by Stephen Morley

A CIP catalogue record for this book
is available at the British Library
ISBN 0 413 69270 1

Typeset by Falcon Graphic Art Ltd
Wallington, Surrey
Printed in Spain by Cayfosa,
Barcelona

To Margaret, Ruth, Gavin, Robyn
and the cast and crew of
Pat and Margaret, with thanks

The M6 motorway. The traffic churns by. At the Kirkby Preston Motorway Service Area All-Day Breakfast counter, Margaret tips out her last tin of chips and clocks off. At the entrance to the locker-room her workmates are waiting for her, all dressed up. Bella and Sue follow her into the locker-room as she takes off her uniform.

Bella	Come on woman, got a blooming coach revving up outside.
Margaret	No, I were waiting for chips.
Bella	Waiting for chips. Blooming live television show to get to, she's waiting for chips.
Margaret	Well I was.
Bella	Well I was she says. Women! Come on!

Margaret scrambles into a smartish top. She still has her flat work shoes on.

Bella	You're not going in those shoes?
Margaret	They're comfy.

Bella manages to get the women moving.

Sue	Leave her alone, she'll only be sat in the audience, she's not Dame Bloody Kiri Te Sodding Kanawa.

Bella hustles them outside and on to the coach. Margaret stops to talk to Jim, her boyfriend.

Margaret	Bella's still got a ticket. Could you not come?
Jim	Better not. My mother and so forth.
Margaret	Oh well. Where are you mopping, Gents?
Jim	There's been an overflow, Level Two urinals Southbound. They bleeped me over from Northbound.
Margaret	You're in demand with that mop.
Jim	We have it to do.
Margaret	So is that all right then, picking us up after?
Jim	Roger wilco, I'll be there.
Bella	*(calling from the coach)* Mrs Woman, get on!
Margaret	Well I might be too famous to talk to you by then!
Jim	Oh, what, the telly?
Margaret	See ya!

Margaret boards the coach. Jim gazes after her. The door shuts and the engine starts. Jim mouths through the window.

Jim   What's it called?
Margaret Pardon?
Bella   Speak up Rambo!

Jim   The television — business — what's it called?

Everyone sings out, to the famous TV signature tune:

All   *Magic Moments!*

The coach pulls away, to a cheer from the women.

1958. A street of grey pebble-dashed council houses. Pat, aged seven, parades up the street in a skimpy ruched swimming-costume, sunglasses, beads and her mother's high heels. Margaret, aged two, watches from her tricycle, holding an ice-cream. Pat clops past her and snatches up the ice-cream. Margaret looks at her but doesn't say anything.

Heathrow Airport, International Arrivals. The press are hanging around. Billy, a middle-aged photographer, looks up and puts his liquorice allsorts away.

Billy Sweets away, boys, get flashing.

Up sweeps Pat, gleaming, groomed and glamorous, surrounded by a bevy of airline officials, and Claire, her very pregnant forty-year-old PA. Claire is holding Pat's bag, make-up case, coat and flowers. The press break into a chorus of:

Press Over here, Miss Bedford.
One for me, Miss Bedford. (*Etc., etc.*)

Pat carefully favours each camera while giving the impression of keeping moving. She takes from Claire a copy of her book My Life in 'Glamor' *and poses with it.*

Pat Really boys, you're very naughty, I know I'm going to be on the front page of every paper tomorrow looking a complete don't know what!

Billy Good to be back, Pat?

Pat (*sweeping away*) I'm English darling, this is home – football, Marmite, the Queen Mum . . . (*Her smile drops as she leaves the press behind.*) . . . filth, beggars, no choice of lettuce . . .

Peacock Studios. Our coach pulls up outside and the girls spill out. Bella tries to check them as they mill about. Margaret wanders off to admire the scene.

Bella Now everybody's to stick with me. We've to queue at Door 4. Where's Margaret gone now? Margaret!

Margaret turns and smiles and is seized by an irate Bella.

Bella	Will you stick to the party, lady!
Margaret	I'm just looking out for celebrities.
Bella	Don't show me up, come on.
Margaret	This is great, isn't it?
Bella	Yes, it's fandabidozie. Come on!

A corridor, Peacock Studios. Bella's girls head the Magic Moments *queue. The queue is mainly composed of middle-aged and elderly women. The girls stare at the huge framed photos on the walls.*

Margaret	Is that Michael Barrymore?
Sue	What are you like? That's him off news. Michael Barrymore!

Daisy, a young researcher with a clipboard, has a quick word with the security man and approaches the queue.

Daisy	Party leader? Mrs Franklyn?
Bella	This is my party.
Daisy	Could I have a word?

The girls pull faces at each other.

Sue	What do you bet we've got wrong tickets.
Margaret	We haven't have we?
Sue	Or not enough − they're saying − everyone except her in t'anorak.
Margaret	They are not.
Daisy	(*to Bella*) No, that's fine. We just needed to know she was actually on the premises.
Bella	No, that were plain sailing, really.
Daisy	Is she the little dark one?
Bella	No, the one in blue, with the perm.
Daisy	Oh.
Bella	Why?
Daisy	No, I mustn't say, really I mustn't say a word.

Heathrow Arrivals. Pat stands on the travelator, her entourage behind her. Two lady fans run alongside the travelator, handing out albums of photos and autograph books.

First fan	Miss Bedford, Miss Bedford! We wrote to you in LA! We're the two diabetics from Ketteridge!
Pat	Pen!

Claire hands over a pen.

Second fan	We won't be back in time for *Magic Moments* but we're taping it. We've ordered the book.
Pat	Sweet of you.
First fan	We never miss *Glamor.* I was once mistaken for you at a traffic-light.
Pat	Oh.
Second fan	Is it true they're going to axe the series?
Pat	No.
First fan	(*holding out large envelope*) Would it be possible to have a twelve-by-eight colour portrait to Kay and Bunty?
Pat	Claire.

Claire takes the envelope. The fans fall behind a little.

First fan	Good luck with *Magic Moments*!
Second fan	We loved you in *Lakeland Vet.*
First fan	We do your workout!
Second fan	Do you have any message for diabetics?

They fall behind, panting.

Pat	When you deal with me, Claire, think icon.

The Magic Moments studio. Most of the audience is seated. Bella's party file into their seats, helped by an usher. Margaret is about three seats in from the aisle. The floor manager nods in response to a message in his earpiece and goes to rearrange them, putting Margaret on the aisle.

Sue   Blimey, what does it matter, they're not numbered seats.

A dressing room, Peacock Studios. Pat sweeps in with Claire, snatches the make-up case and plonks it down on the counter in front of Nadia, the make-up girl.

Nadia   Sorry, what do you want me to do with this?
Pat   Put it on me.

An office in a newspaper building, that evening. Stella, a glamorous fiftyish journalist, all big hair and bracelets, is setting her video with a bar-code scanner. On one wall is a poster plugging Stella as Columnist of the Year. There is also a framed book cover, the back of which is a photo of Stella; the front says 'Life in the Shadows, the unauthorised biography of Cliff Richard'. She speaks into a little tape recorder.

Stella   Yes — idea for Pat Bedford book, chapter four. Maybe analyse a typical interview, like the *Magic Moments*, break it down for grammar, vocabulary, content, really try and expose the ignorant little tart beneath the veneer.

Pat's dressing-room. Pat is having her make-up touched up by Nadia. Claire stands close by.

Nadia   Have you seen *Magic Moments*, Miss Bedford?

Pat   No. *(To Claire's stomach.)* Could you move that?

Claire   Sorry. I had a scan today. *(She thrusts the photo in front of Pat.)* You can see his spine.

Pat   I don't care if you can see the washing instructions on his underpants. Do the job. Not interested.

Nadia   This is gorgeous powder, Miss Bedford. I don't know this brand.

Pat   I have it specially blended for me in Vagina — Geneva.

Jim's house. An extremely neat and tidy living-room. His mum is stuffing a knitted animal with kapok. Jim is hovering about.

Mum   What's the matter with you, stop looming!

Jim   Will you be having the television on at all?

Mum   When I've stuffed this penguin to my own satisfaction, possibly.

The Magic Moments *studio. Cameras are moving into position. Martin, the dapper warm-up man, is roaming up and down aisles with his hand-held radio mike, jollying everyone up.*

Martin   I think I'll come down here now, I'm fed up with you lot! Only kidding, you're a marvellous bunch. All righty, where's our party from the Chestnuts Home for the Elderly, Washwood Heath?

There's a cheer from a group of old ladies.

And we have a Mrs Maisie Stephenson, she's ninety-two years young today! Whoo!

Cheers and applause.

She's sitting over there with her mum and dad! No, only kidding, that's marvellous.

Old folks' home, Lancashire. A helper pushes a row of old ladies into position in front of the TV.

Helper   Are you going to watch it, Vera? This is the programme Aggie was going to be on if she hadn't have died.

A corridor outside the Magic Moments *studio. Pat in full slap and costume, pacing up and down, rehearsing her anecdotes. Claire stands by with Pat's paraphernalia.*

Pat   And this is another story I tell in the book — when I was invited to the Emmys, and I wore a dress that was so tight, you could see me changing my mind. The dress was so tight Maeve — you could see me changing my mind!

Round the corner at full pelt comes Maeve, also in full slap but with curlers and trainers, followed by Daisy, holding Maeve's evening shoes. Pat and Maeve kiss, without touching.

Maeve	Pat! You look fabulous! Was the flight OK? Are you worn out? You'll have to give me your diet, I'm getting like an old washerwoman here.
Pat	Well, it's all in my book!
Maeve	That's great. I'll get my head combed out and I'll catch you on set later. It's a bundle of fun − it goes like a rocket. You look gorgeous. (*She bustles away and murmurs to Daisy.*) She's getting very haggard.

Magic Moments *studio.*

| Martin | And he said, never mind that, who bombed our chip shop? Nice one that, isn't it. (*He checks his list and moves down a few steps.*) Now. Where are the ladies of the Kirkby Preston Service Area Cafeteria Serving Staff? |

Bella's girls cheer and wave.

	You're the girls dishing up the curly sandwiches and the old burnt bangers eh?
Bella	(*off mike*) It's very good food.
Martin	(*points his mike at her*) What's that, my darling?
Bella	I say it's very good food these days, Martin.
Martin	Slap my wrist. I know it is, my sweetheart. Only kidding. They do a marvellous job on these motorways, don't they everybody?

Back in the corridor. Pat is in a rage. Daisy is caught in the crossfire.

Pat   Do you keep all your American stars waiting in corridors? Is this how Bob Hope would be treated, or Shirley MacLaine? I am the biggest soap star on American television, do you know what I was doing last night? I was dueting, in harmony, with Liza Minnelli and Macaulay Culkin.

Daisy   Erm — sorry — it's unavoidable.

Pat   No. What's your name?

Daisy   Daisy.

Pat   No, Daisy. It's not unavoidable. There is never a good reason for malatreating a top-rated celebrity, and the sooner you get a grip on that factum, the more likely you'll do so! (*Realising there's half a sentence missing here, she snaps her fingers at Claire.*) Water!

Magic Moments studio.

Martin Well, we're nearly ready to go, let me just remind you one more time — it is a live show, we can't go back and do it again — so if you do get called out by Maeve, and this is a surprise type show, lots of we hope nice surprises in store for one or two of you — if you do get called out — just come straight down, there'll be someone to show you the way — watch your language — no effing and blinding please — no alternative comedy — not nice these days, is it — just got a minute or two to go now. Now, who remembers Lenny the Lion?

Holding area behind the Magic Moments *set. Maeve, now combed out and with her high heels on, very grim and businesslike, is examining a script with Daisy, who holds her trainers.*

Maeve Yeah, OK, so we think they haven't seen each other for twenty-seven years.
Daisy They don't look alike by the way.
Maeve Oh damn, that would have been nice wouldn't it. And they're moving that autocue nearer, yeah?
Daisy Yeah.
Maeve How do you say this? Motters-head?
Daisy Motter-shead I think.
Maeve Mottershead. Margaret Mottershead.

A floor assistant pokes her head round a flat and gives Maeve the thumbs up. Maeve hands her glasses to Daisy.

OK. Mottershead. Mottershead. Oh God, what's first now? The puppy!

The old folks' home. The old ladies stare at the TV as Magic Moments *begins.*

Helper Wake up, Vera. Pat Bedford's on this, you like her, don't you?

Jim's living-room. Jim has the TV on. A lavatory flushes. On the TV screen, Maeve descends a staircase to music and applause. Mum comes in.

Mum What's this? This is never wildlife of the Kalahari.
Jim The girls from work are in the audience.
Mum (*stretching her hand out for the remote*) Don't handle this please, it's all over lavatory cleaner now.

She changes channels, the music changes to desert-type and Jim turns away, defeated.

The holding area. Pat is pacing furiously and shouting at Claire. A meek floor assistant is keeping well out of the way.

Pat   I've been in earthquakes that were better organised than this.

Claire   I think it's just that they don't want anyone in the audience to see you.

Pat   Thank you Claire. You have a lifetime's experience in show business do you? Or is getting pregnant and not tracking down the right bra it?

Magic Moments studio. Bella and her girls are applauding wildly at some sentimental item. Maeve turns to her camera as an old man, Harry, leading a puppy, is led off the set.

Maeve   Wasn't that lovely? And Harry not only gets the puppy but all that lovely dog food.

Margaret Ah! Any chance of me going to the toilet?

Bella   No! Stay put!

Maeve   Now we've had some extraordinary reunions on *Magic Moments* but I think you'll find this one is extra special. It concerns two people — one of the ladies in question thinks she's just here for a night out with the girls — the girls of the Kirkby Preston Motorway Service Area Cafeteria.

Sue, Margaret and the girls all look at each other. Bella stares straight ahead.

Maeve   Yes − step into the limelight − this is your Magic Moment − Margaret Mottershead!

The girls shriek. An usher leads Margaret as she half stumbles down the steps to Maeve, dumping her bag and anorak at the last minute. Martin keeps the applause going. Margaret sits on an adjoining sofa to Maeve, a monitor between them. Behind them is a huge video wall, on which we see a series of old photos.

Maeve	Now tell us who that is, Margaret.
Margaret	My Aunty Aggie – she lived next door.
Maeve	She lived next door to you and your sister. And she looked after you and minded you, whatever.

Margaret nods.

Well she was a big fan of the programme.

Scattered applause.

And she had a bit of a story to tell about you and your sister. We were hoping she'd come and tell us in the studios, but she's dead unfortunately – but anyway . . .

A photo of Pat and Margaret at the ages of six and two comes up on the screen.

There you are now. You're the little one, yes? Love those old woolly costumes don't you? And who's the big girl?

Margaret	That's my sister Pat.

Stella's office. As Margaret says the word 'Pat', Stella is suddenly riveted to the television.

The back of the Magic Moments *set. Pat is ushered by a floor assistant into the studio with Claire. There is a monitor, which Pat is too busy complaining to notice. Daisy hurries to meet Pat.*

Daisy　　Only one second now, I promise.

Pat　　As soon as I get to a telephone, you're fired.

On the set. Margaret sits uncomprehending.

Maeve　　Now Pat and your Mammy didn't get on too well, had a bit of a row, usual thing, and off Pat heads, bright lights and all, whatever.

Margaret stares at her.

And you were what, about ten at the time, and you totally lost touch, you've never seen her from that day to this. A common enough tale on *Magic Moments* but let's take a closer look at that naughty runaway sister Pat.

The back of the set. The floor assistant stands by to lead Pat on.

Pat　　You're very fortunate I'm a consommé professional. Mirror!

Claire hands her a mirror, she checks her cleavage and hands it back. She then notices the monitor, which shows a close-up of Pat aged about nine.

On the set. Margaret stares at the old photo of Pat in a deckchair.

Maeve See anybody you recognise?

The audience is baffled, but some are beginning to cotton on.

How about this?

The shot changes to a publicity photo of Pat aged eighteen, from 1969. The audience gets very excited.

Recognise her now?

The shot changes to Pat as she appears in Glamor. *The audience 'oohs' and 'aahs'. Margaret is frozen.*

Yes! Margaret Mottershead, motorway waitress, the sister you haven't seen for twenty-seven years, now one of the highest paid actresses in American television — a very special Magic Moment — here she is — from *Glamor* — the glamorous — Patricia Bedford.

The audience bursts into wild applause. Pat stands side stage, unable to believe what has happened. Martin and the floor assistant keep the applause going.

Well I know she's here 'cos I saw her round the back when I was in me curlers. Come and meet your sister — Patricia Bedford!

Pat stumbles on to the set as if pushed, recovers herself, takes the applause and goes to Margaret with outstretched arms. Margaret stands up awkwardly. They embrace. Bella and the girls are overcome.

Maeve	Isn't that our best one yet? Well, they've an awful lot of catching up to do, which we'll find out all about next week — meanwhile, back in a couple of minutes with more Magic Moments.

The lights dim to silhouette.

Martin	We're off the air, folks!

Maeve is rushed at by sound men and make-up girls. Pat and Margaret look at each other. Martin is chatting to the audience.

Margaret	Pat?
Pat	*(breaking away)* Sorry, would you excuse me . . .

She turns away, leaving Margaret on the set. The audience flood happily out to the exit. Bella and the girls clatter down the stairs.

Sue	Did you know, you bugger?
Bella	No, I thought she were getting a prize for chip frying or summat.
Sue	Well what now? Is there a do?
Bella	Oh yeah, there must be. Well, we can't all — look, can you get them on the coach, just for now, and I'll go round and ask.

Hospitality — a bare, featureless conference room with a bar and buffet table set up at one end. There are a few production people, Harry and the puppy, and a couple of waitresses. Billy, armed with his camera, is hovering hopefully by the buffet with Daisy.

Daisy	Did you get the studio shots with Pat and her sister?
Billy	They weren't on the floor.
Daisy	Well do them in here then.
Billy	What are those then, vol au vents?
Daisy	Hands off, Billy. We don't take the clingfilm off till Maeve comes.

Maeve sweeps in with her team, high on adrenalin.

| **Maeve** | Well, you'll have to go a long way to beat that one. Did you see their faces, that Margaret, I thought now please nobody die, oh God give us a drink, hi Billy, just head and shoulders tonight eh, I'll never get my shoes back on, it's a pity I'm too grand to soak them in a bucket, get the clingfilm off, let me at the chicken legs — now, what's Pat having? Where is Pat? |

A studio corridor. Pat, thinking furiously, is led by Claire to the lifts. They pass a ladies' toilet.

| **Claire** | Oh golly, I'm sorry, you see his back is right on my bladder — two ticks! |

Claire nips in and Pat turns round and goes back to the studio.

The old folks' home. The helpers are wheeling the old ladies out. One, Vera, is very agitated and pointing at the screen.

Helper	Come on Vera, coming for cocoa?
Vera	It was my Pat! My Pat!
Helper	What say, Vera?
Vera	That was her, I recognise her now — it's my little girl!

The helpers look at each other, not sure how to take this.

The empty studio. Margaret is up in the seating, collecting her bag and brushing the dust off her anorak. Pat comes on to the studio floor. Margaret is thrilled.

| **Margaret** | Hiya! I didn't know where everybody had gone, I didn't know what I was supposed to do — my sister being the one in *Glamor* — I'm gobsmacked, me! |
| **Pat** | Come down here. |

Margaret comes down.

Margaret	'Cos you give me such a funny look before — I had this horrible feeling — erk — she doesn't want me to be here —
Pat	I don't.
Margaret	Pardon?
Pat	I don't want to talk to you.
Margaret	Why not?
Pat	I don't want this. I'm doing a book. I'm here to plug a book.
Margaret	What have I to do then?
Pat	How did you get here?
Margaret	We came on a coach.
Pat	Fine. Go and get on it. I'll deal with everything else.
Margaret	Do you not want to know about me?
Pat	No. I don't want to know.
Margaret	Have I just to go then?

Pat nods. Margaret turns and plods up the steps.

The studio coach park. The coach is full of laughing, chatting girls. Bella climbs on board.

Sue	What's happening?
Bella	You tell me. Margaret's round the back somewhere, they wouldn't let me through.
Sue	Shall we hang on a bit for her?
Bella	Well we can't wait long.

28

Studio corridor. Margaret is lost and starting to panic. She's going along corridors, opening fire doors, wrong doors, doors she's opened before. Claire comes bounding round a corner, holding a few copies of Pat's book.

Claire	Hi! Coming up for a nosh?
Margaret	Do you know where the coach would be?
Claire	The coach?
Margaret	We all came on a coach, I don't want them to leave without me.
Claire	Oh no, you're staying with Pat tonight, well, for as long as —
Margaret	Is that what Pat wants?
Claire	Oh yes, I'm sure — she must be thrilled. Anyway, come on, you're missing the party!
Margaret	Could my friends come? Would that be all right?
Claire	Oh gosh yes! Ask for Hospitality, I'll see you there!
Margaret	I'll go and get them then.

The coach park. Bella stands on the steps of the coach, looking out over the empty park. Margaret sees the coach from the window of the studio building and dashes down. The door is chained, and as Margaret waves and calls, Bella boards the coach and it pulls away.

Pat, a little more relaxed, walks to Hospitality with Claire.

Pat   I get letters from people like that all the time. They're my sister, they're my mother. I'm glamorous, attractive, I have enough sexual charisma to open a factory — she's fat, Northern, working class — of course she wants to be my sister. I absolutely sympathise — life is very tough for these Northern women.

I did a cameo on a Barbara Taylor Bradford — it was heartbreaking. Anyway, she's gone, no harm done — if we can just get that bit edited out, put in an interview concentrating on the book, and ooh la la.

They go through into —

Hospitality.

Claire   No, she's still here — she's coming up to the party with her friends from the motorway.

Pat is greeted by Maeve's merry group as this news sinks in.

Maeve   Pat!

Pat is drawn into the group and given a drink.

I said, didn't I, her and that sister of hers will be having a good old natter somewhere, catching up on the old times — what a story! They had some trouble digging it up; you're as close as a clam with the old personal info — now where's the Margaret woman?

Pat   I'll just get Claire to fetch her. Excuse me a moment.
Daisy   Harry with the dog, wasn't that sweet.

They continue with the shop talk as Pat snatches her bag from Claire and takes out some cash.

Pat   Stop her coming in here. Give her this and get her to go.
Claire What should I say, she was awfully thrilled. I mean I thought she seemed terribly nice.
Pat   Take it and do it. Roger! (*She turns back to the crowd.*)

An empty tea bar. Almost deserted, it's obviously not where the party is. Margaret sits alone. A large West Indian lady behind the till looks at her suspiciously.

Tea lady   We don't serve you.
Margaret   No, I'm just — (*She straightens the salt and pepper.*) I like your till.

Claire dashes in. Margaret stands up in relief.

Margaret	I didn't know where anybody was, I was just thinking — this probably isn't the right place is it?
Claire	I've just had a wee word with Pat.
Margaret	The coach went.
Claire	She just wondered if I could give you this!
Margaret	You see — I don't have any way of getting home now.
Claire	Right.
Margaret	So what about staying with Pat — is that still on? — otherwise I'm a bit lumbered.
Claire	No, that's absolutely —

They start to move off. Margaret is relieved.

Margaret	'Cos I don't know the set-up. I don't know Pat. I've not seen her since I was ten — there's not much in it for her, me turning up!

Hospitality.

Pat	Now I do have to go rather shortly, it's been a very long flight, and a very long day.
Maeve	Oh God yes, understood.
Pat	And my people will be talking to your people, but I'm afraid there's been somewhat of a virago.

Maeve	A what?
Daisy	Farrago?
Maeve	Fandango? Façade?
Pat	The sister thing.
Maeve	The Magic Moment?
Pat	The part where you brought on the sister — I wonder how much of an upheaval would it be to edit that part out.
Maeve	Take your bit out?
Pat	Yes.
Maeve	No problem. In fact, we'll give you the whole thing. Daisy would have sent you a tape anyway.
Pat	Yes, thank you — but no — I meant — take that bit out of the programme altogether — not show it.
Maeve	Well it's a nice idea, there's lots of things I'd like to go back and do again —
Pat	Oh, so you could —
Maeve	The nice thing about it being live, we don't have to worry about it — it's over —
Pat	It's live? It's already been out?
Maeve	We went live in ninety-two, you have been away a long time.

Claire comes in with Margaret.

Maeve	Margaret, for heaven's sake. Will you get yourself outside a glass of champagne before it all goes. Let's have a toast to sisters!
Pat and Margaret	Sisters!

Billy snaps their pose.

Billy	Lovely. Any chance of a kiss?

Pat's suite, Regent Hotel. The doors are flung open with a flourish by a manager, followed by Pat, two sweating porters, Claire, Margaret and a publicity lady. A maid is scuttling about doing flowers etc.

Margaret is drawn into the suite, which is huge and over-decorated, covered in flowers. She stands open-mouthed while Pat goes into overdrive. The poor maid gets drawn into it all.

Pat	I want everything unpacked and the Chanel, the St Laurent and the Issey Miyake pressed immediately. *Comprehendé?* Bring them back the second the work is completed; as an icon, I'm very vulnerable and I don't wish my under or outer wear to be a target for perverts' hand relief. Yes? *Si? Oui-oui?* That lamp lit, that one dimmed, TV to CNN . . .

They all scuttle round. She scans a menu.

	Four ounces of freshly squeezed organic grape juice, skinless chicken on granary no animal fat and an 'erb tea.
Manager	Anything else I can do to help, Miss Bedford?
Pat	No. Claire, drapes, close. You — put that in the bathroom and everyone else can leave now.

They all disappear through various doors. Margaret wanders off to inspect the other rooms.

Pat	Well?
Claire	Er, sorry?
Pat	Thanks to your umbilical incompetence, I, sexy yet vulnerable, and I'm quoting from *Harper's* here, I, Pat Bedford, of *Glamor*, have been exposed on nationwide television as having some dubious connection with an overweight Northern waitress with all the sophisticated allure of an airline salad. I, who came sixth in the World's Most Envied Bottom poll, 1992 — only two below Claudia Schiffer — am now publicly linked to a woman whose buttocks practically skim the carpet.
Claire	But she's so nice — and she's having such a lovely time.

Pat	I gave you fifty pounds to give her and tell her to go. Did you give it to her? Did she leave? No. Have I had the money back? No.
Claire	(*fumbling in her bag*) But I just kept thinking if my baby had a sister, and if they got separated, and if somebody gave my baby fifty pounds not to see my other baby —
Pat	Yes, and if I had a penis and a hairy chest I could play Hamlet, King Lear and Robin Prince of Thieves. I can't afford to have her here. You know *Glamor*'s dropped down from the top spot; any excuse, any hint of a scandal we'll be off the air, or even worse, on the air without me. I'm Valerie Lady Charleson, I'm Knightsbridge, I'm grooming, I'm camisoles. I can't be seen to have a blood relative with a Lancashire accent and a perm you could go trick-or-treating in.
Claire	But I don't think she'd —
Pat	It looks wrong. It's not me. Oh — come early and help me get rid of her — before the press call.
Claire	I'll . . . OK . . . I'll get a cab then . . . I think she's so nice . . .

Pat, not listening, is changing channels and cramming grapes into her mouth. Claire tries to leave.

Pat	Oh and Claire — when handling drapes, don't drag them manually — it's very bad for the fabric — use the pulleys provided. (*She demonstrates.*) Like so, and so.

Margaret taps at an inner door and comes in, smiling.

Margaret	Do you knock or not, I didn't know. They don't tell you that one do they, in t'magazines. Do you knock door of famous sister you haven't seen for twenty-seven years? Or do you not knock? Blooming heck though, this. I mean what is it like? There's pot-pourri on the top of the toilet in there, that would be four pounds in a shop. Even on the market that would be four pounds. And the pillows on the bed! Eight pillows! This thick! Make mine look like cream crackers! Sorry — I'm going on. It's the champagne — I could never see why they went on about it before.
Pat	I'm going to bed.
Margaret	Yes, I'm sorry. I'm worn out and I've only come on t'motorway. I can't really phone Bella now, can I. I'll phone them at work tomorrow.
Pat	Don't call anybody.
Margaret	Fair enough. I'll get to bed then as well. Are them shower caps free, do you know?
Pat	Yes, it's all free.
Margaret	Oh, terrific. Night then. Oh — the only thing is, 'cos I didn't know I was coming, I've no pants.
Pat	Pants?
Margaret	Clean pants for tomorrow. Tights I can rinse through —

Pat leaves. Margaret follows her to the doorway and takes the tiny pair of lacy pants Pat holds out.

	Oh ta.
Pat	I have to go to bed.
Margaret	Don't worry about what you said to me before, about wanting me to go. I'd only come to watch the show — I wasn't expecting blooming sister to come crawling out the woodwork, I wasn't that thrilled myself to tell you the honest truth. I was thinking oh blimey last time I saw her she smacked me across the face. Do you remember?
Pat	No. Look — I must —

She starts to close the door on Margaret.

Margaret	Oh — what time's breakfast? What time have we to be down by?

The door closes.

The Kirkby Preston Motorway Services. It's late. The coach pulls up at the Staff Entrance. Bella and a couple of the other women wearily get out. Jim looms up out of the shadows. Bella walks to her car.

Bella	Oh, it's you.
Jim	Wasn't Margaret being dropped off here — was that not the arrangement?
Bella	Did you not see it?
Jim	No, my mother wanted the wildlife.
Bella	Yes, well she's Pat Bedford's sister seemingly.
Jim	Sorry?
Bella	Her in *Glamor*. Valerie Lady Charleson. Oh, come on, she's in every paper out.
Jim	I can't read, so I'm not so hot on the names. Faces — fine.
Bella	Look, I'm matt lacquered, all right? All I know is she's teamed up with Pat Bedford, we haven't had a word from her and she's stayed up London.
Jim	Oh. Was there no message for me?
Bella	None for you, me or anybody. So we'll see. 'Night. (*She drives off.*)

The front of the Regent Hotel, early next morning. A small crowd of press is hanging about. Billy is handing round coffees in a box lid. Parked close by, Stella is standing by her car looking at an envelope of photos, shots of Pat and Margaret from last night. Billy comes over with a coffee for Stella.

Stella	Thanks darling. You were wearing that tie on the *Leicester Mercury*.
Billy	Probably was as well.
Stella	Yes, these are nice. I'll take these.
Billy	Oh cheers. Well I'm around all weekend if you want any more.
Stella	She's cancelled my interview. I thought it was worth a try. Any sign of the sister?
Billy	Neither of them. She's not taking any calls.
Stella	Well this is all jolly intriguing. Very nice for little Stella's book.

Pat's hotel room. Pat, fully made up in a very glamorous tracksuit, is doing a workout to her own workout video. The Pat on the tape is very flatteringly lit and surrounded by hunky young men. She low-impacts over to the window and sees the press is all still there.

Margaret's room. She dials a number.

Margaret Oh hello Mrs Dench, it's Margaret here. Margaret Mottershead. I tried to get hold of Jim at work but – could you give him a message for me? Can you say I'm sorry about last night, it got too late to phone, and I'm not sure what I have to do here, but I'll come home as soon as I can. I don't think I'll be staying very long, I don't think Pat – well, I miss him loads tell him, and I'll be home soon. Can you pass that on, please? Bye.

The hall of Jim's house. His mum puts the phone down. Jim thunders down the stairs half dressed.

Jim Was that Margaret? Is she having a nice time?
Mum Your Aunty Ivy wanting wool.

Jim turns to go back upstairs.

Your label's out on your vest.

Pat's room. Margaret pokes her head round the door.

Margaret   Hiya! The girl who brought my coffee said you've got more journalists outside than José Carreras — can't be bad.

Pat freezes the frame.

Pat   I'm waiting for Claire, she has my bag, and then I will write you a cheque.
Margaret   Pardon?
Pat   Just a one-off payment.
Margaret   No, I'm fine. I got paid yesterday. There was overtime — I'm fine.
Pat   This won't be a regular thing. I'm already heavily committed charitywise — tropical fish for shut-ins, evening dresses for single mothers —
Margaret   Sorry, you've lost me.
Pat   So a one-off payment. You sign this, it's just to say we're not related, you're not my sister, you have no claim on Pat Bedford Inc., that's my company.
Margaret   I'm not signing that.

Pat	What?
Margaret	I am your sister. You know I am. You recognised me straight away, didn't you.
Pat	Don't sign it till Claire brings the cheque – I'm not trying to be unreasonable.
Margaret	I don't want the cheque. I haven't got a bank account anyway. I had a surprise last night as well, you know. I didn't want to stay. I could have been on a coach last night having a laugh, could have been at work this morning, not stuck in a room all on my own, having croissants which I don't even like.
Pat	Fine. Go back. But don't go out the front.
Margaret	Why, 'cos of the journalists?
Pat	They twist things.
Margaret	There's nothing to twist about me. Met up with a long lost sister, long lost sister didn't want to know, went home.
Pat	There's probably a back way through the kitchens.
Margaret	Oh well, I'll feel very comfy there then, won't I? It's very me, is kitchens. Oh and here's your pants. Don't worry – I didn't wear them. I washed mine and put them on the towel rail.
Pat	Have them.
Margaret	No thanks. I don't want anything of yours.

She opens the door and in sails Claire followed by a camera crew.

Claire	Morning! This is John, Mike and Sarah. They're doing the *Magic Moments* follow-up film, did I mention it?
Pat	No.
Claire	They'll be following you and Margaret round all day, loads of fun things planned.

The freeze-frame unfreezes.

Pat	(*on video*) And give those buns one last squeeze. Relax, you deserve it.
Claire	So, what shall we do? A little bit of filming in here?
Pat	Yes.
Claire	Suppose Pat and Margaret both do the exercise video. Would that be fun?

The lounge of the Regent Hotel. Pat is giving a press conference, plugging her book and workout video. Stella is very much in the background, whispering to Billy. Margaret is doing a piece to her own camera crew.

Margaret	This is a press conference right, the press are wanting to know about Pat's book, and me, and what I do, all of that. And so far, I'm having a wonderful time! Margaret Mottershead, Regent Hotel, Marylebone, London, the World!
Pat	I have chips, I have chocolate, I pig out, pig out, pig out, but I always have my mango – it's enzymes – all very proven and above hand.
Billy	Margaret? How have your friends on the Motorway taken to all this?
Margaret	I haven't had a chance to speak to them yet, not even got hold of my boyfriend yet!
Billy	He's a lav cleaner, isn't he dear? How do you think he'd take to the Californian lifestyle?
Margaret	He'd probably hate it. I don't know, he can't read, so new places are difficult. I'd like it though, given the chance!

| Stella | Planning to look up family and friends in the North while you're here, Pat? |
| | |

Pat knows exactly who Stella is, but keeps cool.

Pat	No, it's a very crammed schedule unfortunately.
Stella	So, your mother won't be expecting a visit?
Pat	I'm afraid she's no longer with us. But I'm sure she's looking down from somewhere − dear old Vera − sorry, could we leave it there, it's rather upsetting, I miss her now . . .

The conference starts to break up, as Pat seems near to tears.

Stella	I had a little phone call yesterday.
Billy	Oh yeah?
Stella	There's a Vera in an old folks' home in Pat's home town. Fancy a little tripette?

Followed by their crew, Pat and Margaret visit an exclusive clothes shop where nothing fits Margaret, and a diner where Pat struggles to make chips.

They finish their little film by the pool in a health club. Pat and Margaret, both in fluffy robes, are dangling their toes in the water. Margaret has had her hair and face done.

Margaret	(*shyly*) Well, Pat, LA sounds wonderful.
Pat	Darling, you'll adore it, and with all your gorgeous down-to-earth Northern charm they will adore you! (*She drops her smile and looks past the camera.*) OK?
John	Thank you. That's it, we're done.
Pat	Was the bit about my three houses OK? I would hate to sound ontenstatious. I must get out of this tacky robe. Claire!

44

The Motorway Services kitchen, the same day. Bella, in uniform, surrounded by the usual girls, is talking earnestly to Stella, while Billy snaps away.

Bella   The thing is, Stella, we've heard nothing since she got off the coach — I mean how difficult is it to pick up a phone? Apart from her being a mate ho ho, I've got rosters to organise, there's people queuing up to do shift work here — do I hold it open or what?

Stella   Very difficult for you. Now where can I find Jim?

The health club. Pat, Claire and the crew are leaving. Margaret, red-faced and hair ruined from the sauna, is fumbling with her bag and purse and anorak at the pay phone. When she sees them leaving she gives up on the call and dashes after them, but is caught on the wrong side of a fish-pond and can't catch up.

Jim's living-room. The tea trolley is laden, and Mum is in full swing.

Mum   You see she's not phoned, Stella, no consideration for Jim's feelings. Well it smacks very casual, have an Easter Bakewell.

Stella   No, I'm full of, what was it — bap?
Jim   To be fair —
Mum   I'm talking, thank you. Because Jim is illiterate — we make no bones over it. They didn't have dyslexia in those days, you sat at the back with raffia.
Stella   You must feel a little bit sore over this.
Jim   Well, obviously I would like to talk to Margaret on a face to face basis.
Stella   Absolutely. Now, you're a lovely lav cleaner, aren't you? Could we do a few shots with the lavatory? Would there be one indoors, or . . . ?

Pat's suite. Pat lounges on a sofa, on the telephone. A maid is delivering fresh flowers and bottled water.

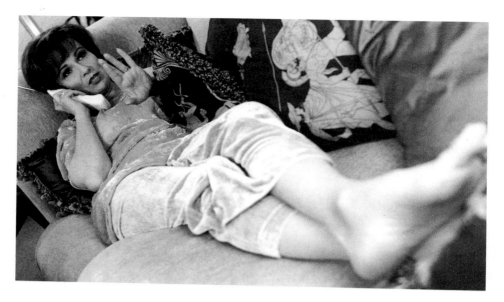

Pat   Well Britain is a grubby little third-rate island, darling, but the point is — they love me. And, this terrible firago with the relative from hell has actually been rather a bonus. (*Listens.*) Yes, quite — (*She clicks her fingers at the maid.*) Chicken? *Pollet*? *Poulenté*? Small portion no skin and nine grapes.

Margaret comes in, unnoticed, as the maid scuttles out.

I mean who needs eight Vietnamese babies when you can have a lumpy old short-order waitress for one week only. Oh no — I'll milk it for all it's worth this week, then I'll go home and she can take a flying — yes quite — at a deep fat fryer! Oh, she's horrendous — the perm, the funny voice — I mean it's real Tracey Ullman time. (*She sees Margaret.*) Yes? I'm talking.

Margaret goes through to her room.

OK darling, and tell them at the meeting Valerie Lady Charleson is red hot in England, she wants some bloody good story-lines next season. *Ciao.*

Early Sunday morning. A paper-girl shoves papers into the letterbox of Jim's house. In the kitchen, Jim is having his breakfast. His mum stabs a finger at the Sunday paper.

Mum   You'll recognise that word, 'Margaret'.

Jim   Yes.

Mum   'It's bye bye Motorway, hello LA, she laughed. There is nothing and no one to keep me here, meeting up with Pat again has been a real godsend.'

Bella's hall. Bella, in rather unglamorous nightwear, has just picked up the paper.

Bella   (*shouting*) 'Meeting Pat again has been a godsend. The job is rubbish, it's hey hey LA for me.'

Sunday morning, the Kirkby Arms Hotel restaurant, Lancashire. Stella, Billy and a stringer from the local paper sit over breakfast with the nationals.

Stella   That's made a nice little column, you see. Bolshy Bella and Jilted Jim. 'Too slow for fast food.'

Stringer   Did she actually say that?

Stella   Snap on dear. Now – Pat Bedford. What have you got for me?

Stringer   Well a lot of the old files were fire-damaged. I've got her old address, school, few bits and bobs. The address of the mother's nursing home is in there.

Stella   Oh well, thanks darling. Oh, and did you dig out any local scandals?

Billy	Eh?
Stella	Well if we have to be in the bloody North darling, I might as well get a column or two out of it.
Billy	Terrible marmalade.
Stringer	Well, there's the man who kept the dogs in the dark with no —
Stella	No dogs. Done dogs to death.
Stringer	There's the baby boom faulty condom thing.
Stella	Mm.
Stringer	This Spanish Villa thing's a big thing here. A local couple built an apartment complex over a chemical dump — no one can get their money back, little old couples have lost their life savings.
Stella	Well, give me the files, I'll have a look through. (*She slaps some money on the table.*) Give me a receipt for that, could you. Come on Bill, let's get to the old folks' home before they all do. Fancy tipping off two papers — you can't trust anybody.

Pat's bathroom, Sunday morning. Pat, admiring herself in the papers, sees one photo she's not so keen on and goes to check her neck in the mirror. Margaret comes in in her anorak.

Margaret	I'm just going for a walk or something. We're not doing anything till this afternoon are we?
Pat	No. Would you have your neck done if you were me?

Margaret	If I were you I'd have a personality transplant.
Pat	You see I do this every day. (*She pulls up her bottom lip.*) And I think that does actually stop it sagging. Be too late for you.
Margaret	Are we in the papers?

50

Pat	Every single one. Look — my legs on this one are just gorgeous.
Margaret	Jim gets this paper. Well his mum reads it to him. What's this — I never said the job was rubbish. They've made half of this up. (*She snatches up another paper.*) That's Bella, they've been talking to Bella.

Bella's hall. Bella is still riveted by the papers.

Bella	'I have no reason to keep the job open. Margaret is no loss, quite frankly, she is too slow for fast food.' I never said that. They've picked that bit out in big letters.

Jim's kitchen.

Mum	These bigger letters here say 'Too slow for fast food'.
Jim	Now that's not fair.
Mum	Shall I read you what it says about you again?
Jim	No.
Mum	'Lavatory attendant. Jim who has learning difficulties' — that's nice —
Jim	Is there a phone number?
Mum	In the paper? For Pat Bedford? She'd be inundated with trouser fumblers. Remember Mrs Anglesey, and the post office window? She was only trying to sell a divan.
Jim	Does it say where they're staying?

Mum	The Regent Hotel. Marylebone Road.
Jim	What road?
Mum	Marylebone. Mary-le-bone.
Jim	Marylebone.
Mum	Where are you off to?
Jim	There. Marylebone Road. You've got Ivy coming. I'll be back in time to open the corned beef. Please Mum, all right?

Pat's suite. Margaret collects her bag and checks her pockets.

Margaret	You see I don't think I've even got Bella's number. Anyway, I'm hopeless on the phone. Where is it the coaches go from, is it Victoria? You wouldn't know.
Pat	(*still admiring her newspaper photos*) What?
Margaret	I'll go straight to the coach station. I'll go to Jim's first, no, Bella's first. You see they don't have to give you notice now, we're all on those funny shift contracts.
Pat	But it's the little telly thing this afternoon.
Margaret	Well I can't do it.
Pat	It's television.
Margaret	Well this is my job. I have a life too you know. I might be just a waitress with a perm and a funny voice, but I can remember when you were a waitress with the same voice and you were pretty pleased with yourself to be one.
Pat	Look, I'll call Claire. She can call Jim, is it, and Bella. She'll smooth the whole thing over.
Margaret	Oh don't be so flipping thick. What's Claire got to do with Bella — just 'cos you can't exist without Claire; even the Queen carries her own handbag you know.
Pat	Just stay a couple more days. It's *Hello!* magazine on Monday. Hampstead Heath remember? The eight-page spread and the leopard-skin leggings? Go on.
Margaret	I thought you were going to say 'please' then. That'd be worth a front page picture.
Pat	Please.
Margaret	Oh come on. I might be daft but I'm not stupid. You had me halfway out through the kitchens yesterday morning, a film crew come on the doorstep and suddenly I'm our delicious Margaret with my lovely Northern charm.

Pat	Well, that's show business. Suit yourself. I can have a virus, fly back early.
Margaret	Right. No harm done then.
Pat	Want a memento of your fifteen minutes of fame? An Andy Warhol quote, you won't have heard of him, he wasn't very big in catering.

She folds up a paper to give Margaret and suddenly freezes.

Margaret	What's the matter?

Pat points to a paragraph.

	What?
Pat	Vera. Little paragraph about Vera.

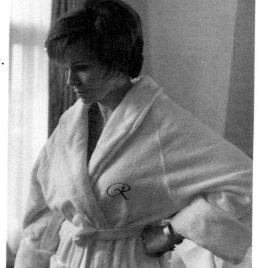

Margaret	What?
Pat	That she's in a nursing home, up there.
Margaret	I never thought she was dead.
Pat	No, but they'll find her.
Margaret	Who?
Pat	Any of them! Stella Kincaid. She was there yesterday. She's trying to get something on me, I'm sure.
Margaret	She's only an old woman, Vera — where's the harm?
Pat	They'd see her. They'd see her and then see me. They'd think I was like her. I hate her. I can't let her do it to me twice.
Margaret	What?

Pat	I can't let her ruin it all, make everything dirty again. I'm not that person now. She doesn't know me.
Margaret	She might not even want to talk to them.
Pat	Oh come on. They pay thousands. Don't you think she'd talk? The woman who did it standing up for ten Bensons.
Margaret	And lying down for twenty.
Pat	It would finish me. Photo this size – some stinking old biddy with a crocheted blanket watching the test card. '*Glamor* Star's Mother in Council Home Hell.' And that's before they've heard her side of the story. I'll have to find her. I'll have to find her before they do.
Margaret	And what, ask her not to say anything?
Pat	Pay her not to say anything. When did she ever do anything for nothing? Not for me. Do you remember how she was?
Margaret	I remember all of it.
Pat	I'll call Claire. No, we can't go crawling around in that huge limo, not round there. Will you come with me?
Margaret	God, I don't want to see her.
Pat	I don't know which nursing home. I don't know her surname. People know me, I can't go round asking questions.
Margaret	Wear a wig. Take Claire.
Pat	This is all private stuff. This is horrible, secret, stuffed away – this is the stuff in the back of the wardrobe. I daren't go on my own.
Margaret	Is this all real or what?
Pat	Yes. Please. And once we've choked her off, I'll get you to Bella's and Jim's – and I'll explain how it is to them. Really, I can sort it out for you.
Margaret	All right.
Pat	I mean we are sisters.
Margaret	We're two middle-aged women in a mess, you mean.

The hotel foyer. Pat, in a wig and what she would consider casual clothes, is on the phone.

Pat	I don't know whether it's worth waiting for Claire anyway. By the time she's fannied about with her nipple shells and her maternity knickers — Claire? Yes, cancel the TV, I don't know about tomorrow yet — Look — we'll go now — you follow us up with the bags and meet us — shut up — What's the biggest hotel?
Margaret	Kirkby Arms, I suppose.
Pat	Meet us in the Kirkby Arms this evening. Don't book me in, I'll be incognito. The Kirkby Arms — I used to drink port and lemon in there.
Porter	The car's outside, Miss Bedford. The keys are in.
Margaret	What's the matter?
Pat	Stella went North yesterday — come on!

Outside the hotel. They climb into a small saloon.

Pat   I don't believe this! Gears! It's not an automatic. This bloody country! Good
Christ, is it not hard enough pointing a car in the right direction without
fiddling with a great big stiff knob at the same time. Can you drive one of these?
Margaret   Not exactly.

Stella and Billy go down the front steps of the old folks' home.

Billy   Well, there we go. Home?
Stella   Oh no darling. I've got lots of little leads in my folder. I haven't nearly finished
with black pudding country yet.

*The M6 motorway. Jim's car whizzes along. A green-lettered strip over the
windscreen says 'JIM' and 'MARGRARET'. As his car passes the Services, Pat's
car jerks and stutters and pulls in on the opposite side.*

*Motorway Services. Pat waits by the Ladies with a couple of drinks and a sandwich.
She's reading the labels as Margaret joins her. They head back for the car, passing a
young family all screaming and throwing food about.*

Pat   They should video that if they want people to use condoms.
Margaret   Perhaps they're tired from travelling.

Pat's car. They drive a little way along the motorway in silence.

Margaret   I was having a baby once. It never went the full — they probably have more
equipment now. Funny year. Gary died in the June, and then I lost her in the,
well, it was about now.
Pat   Were you married then?

56

Margaret	Yeah. He had an accident at work. I was going to get compensation, there was some reason why I didn't.
Pat	I don't know why people have children.
Margaret	Do you not have any?
Pat	No. And my friends don't have any. And my dogs don't have any. All very civilised.

Stella and Billy doorstep on Pat's old estate. They photograph her school, talk to her old neighbours.

The front of the Regent Hotel. As the porter loads the bags into Claire's car, Jim pulls up and parks happily under the ABSOLUTELY NO PARKING *sign. He dashes in.*

| Porter | Oi! Can't you read? |

| Jim | No. |

The porter's desk.

Porter Miss Bedford's car is on the forecourt, madam, the driver's waiting, the bags are in.

Claire Oh good-oh. I'll be two ticks — I absolutely have to spend a penny. Pregnant!

Pat's old house. It is little changed from 1958, but the windows are boarded up. Stella stands outside with the old busybody from next door, who holds a photo album.

Busybody Pregnant at fifteen. Mind you, with a mother like that.

Stella So you knew Vera.

Busybody Everybody knew Vera. Curtains drawn in the afternoon and she wasn't watching Wimbledon. Hang on.

Stella Really.

Busybody We were surprised Pat didn't fall pregnant sooner. I thought — our John took this — that's Vera — now when was that — when did 'Boom Bang-a-Bang' win the Eurovision Song Contest?

Stella Could I borrow this? What did Pat have, an abortion?

Busybody Ooh no, you couldn't get abortions round here then. We didn't get muesli till last year.

58

The porter's desk. Jim stands rather lost by the desk. Claire stops on her way out.

Claire	(*speaking to the receptionist*) Could you pass that on to the switchboard, that's the number, and that's any messages for Miss Bedford, me or Miss Mottershead. Thank you.
Jim	Sorry, did you say Mottershead?
Claire	Yes.
Jim	You're not like a friend of Margaret's are you?
Claire	Well I'm working for Miss Bedford while she's over here.
Jim	I've just like driven down to see Margaret.
Claire	Oh, are you Jim? Oh how ghastly. They've gone north. They went north this morning. You've just come down and they've gone up! Oh what a calamity, what can I do?
Jim	Not to worry, I'll drive back up and track her down.
Claire	Oh, what a bind! Look, how can I help? I think Margaret's so gorgeous . . .

A derelict maternity home on the main road. Stella turns over the original sign, lying in the weeds: SORRENTO MATERNITY HOME, PROP: MRS K. MATHER.

Stella   Must have been grim, mustn't it?
Billy   What now?
Stella   The Red Lion? Do you have to fiddle with your testicles the entire time?

Jim's car. Claire settles herself in as he drives through London.

Claire   No, it's much cosier this way isn't it? I can keep you company, read the road signs, we can have a jolly good old chin-wag.
Jim   Fair enough.
Claire   Though I must warn you, since week seventeen, I've had the most ghastly wind. Real stinkers.

Jim nods gamely, bright red.

The main road. Pat's car passes the maternity home. The car stops.

Margaret   That's not it.

Pat gets out.

That was the unmarried mothers' home – do you remember? We used to see them mopping the front steps.

Pat doesn't answer as she gets out of the car and looks at the derelict building. We hear 'Big Spender' as played on a transistor radio, the voices of young girls laughing and singing.

The hall of the old folks' home. A helper approaches as Pat and Margaret hover. Pat keeps her face away.

Pat	You ask.
Margaret	You ask.
Pat	I'm the celebrity — you ask.
Helper	Yeah?
Margaret	Hello! Do you have a Vera?
Helper	The boiler?
Margaret	No, an old lady.
Helper	Oh, Vera! Yeah. I'll show you. (*She leads the way.*) She never sees nobody normally, you're the second lot today.

Pat winces.

She's down there. In Gladioli. Just past Hyacinth. (*She turns away.*) John! Go and sniff that mince for me!

Pat and Margaret go along the corridor slowly.

Pat I can't go in.

Margaret goes on ahead. She knocks on the door of a two-bedded room. One old lady sits by the door, another stares out of the window.

Margaret   I'm looking for Vera.

The one seated nods at the other.

Old lady   You won't get any sense out of her.
Margaret   Mum? It's Margaret, Mum.

The second old lady, Vera, turns from the window.

Vera   I'm not your mum. My girl's
Julie Andrews. Beautiful Julie.
'Feed the birds, tuppence a bag.'

*Margaret shakes her head at Pat,
who has come as far as the doorway.*

Margaret   It's not her.

They walk slowly away from the room.

Pat	I was dreading seeing her face. I have dreams even now, I've borrowed her blouse, and she's shouting — and — I was so scared then.
Margaret	Even before she turned round I was thinking — it's not her. It just wasn't like Vera.
Pat	Where is she then really? I've got to find her. She can't take it all away from me again.
Helper	Did you get any sense out of her? She's semi-barking most of the time. She were Pat Bedford's mother all last week — that one even got in the papers!

Jim's car. He has relaxed a little and is quite chatty.

Jim	I'd not really come across this PA job before.
Claire	Well a lot of it's very basic in this case. Get Pat to the right place, at the right time with the right bag. Our turn-off next.
Jim	But she's driven up with it herself today. The luggage.
Claire	It's in the limo. I've left them all behind. Oh Crikey Moses.

A petrol station. The forecourt is stacked with logs, plastic cartons and twelve-pound shell suits. Margaret is filling the car with petrol penny by penny, while Pat watches and sips a soft drink.

Pat	Come on.
Margaret	I haven't got much money left you know.
Pat	As soon as I get my bag off Claire —

She sees Billy strolling back to the car with a lolly. Stella is in the car with the door open, scanning her files. Pat drags Margaret out of the way, and they back up behind a car where a girl has all the doors open, shaking her mats. She fiddles with a token, trying to get it in the jet-wash.

Stella   Billy — where's that photo album?
Billy   We back on Vera?
Stella   No, this is the Spanish Villa hoo-ha. You drive, I've just seen the most . . .

Billy drives away. The girl succeeds with the token, the jet-wash starts suddenly and drenches Pat completely.

Pat   I'd like to thank everybody for making this possible. Thank you. Thank you.

Jim's living-room. Claire is coming to the end of a sobbing fit, Mum is in attendance with damp cloths and cups of tea. Jim stands by rather helplessly.

Claire I'm so sorry, I can't believe I've been so stupid, it's my hormones you see, my memory's completely — I don't know what I'm going to do — I have to get Pat's things to the Kirkby Arms this evening.

Jim   The car you were going to come in, could you not ask it to come up with the bags like?

Claire Inspiration! Genius! Of course, I'll phone the hotel. Could I wait here for them, would you mind?

Mum offers a damp cloth.

Claire	Oh thank you. Mm what a lovely smell. Is it lavender?
Mum	It's actually a urinal disinfectant, Jim brings it from work.
Claire	Oh dear, I never cried before I was pregnant, it must be the hormones.
Mum	Oh it will be. I knew a woman that only ate luncheon meat the whole nine months.
Claire	Was the baby all right?
Mum	It was all right then. It ended up selling insurance in Chorlton. So there's no saying, is there.

The very neat garden of a small semi. Mr Lloyd stands in his garden, a FOR
SALE/REPOSSESSION *board up. He's been clipping the hedge. Stella and Billy are
standing on the pavement on the other side of the hedge.*

Mr Lloyd	We'd always liked Spain, and these villas came up, and we thought one for us, one to rent out — we've lost everything basically. My wife can't go out, I don't think she'll recover. Worked all my life, we both have. And there seems to be no redress at all — I've been round their house, to reason with them — it's all dogs and gates, you've no chance. It's not the money so much as what it's done to Mrs Lloyd.

*Pat's old estate. Grey and empty, there's nobody much about. Pat, somehow
managing to look OK in a shell suit, is shouting at Margaret.*

Pat	Is that really all the cash you've got on you?
Margaret	I've bought everything today. And I need most of that for rent.

Pat	Rent?
Margaret	I rent a bedsitter.
Pat	Oh. I'd imagined a little terrace, or a semi.
Margaret	Oh had you. It's a pity I live in real life and not your imagination.
Pat	(*stopping*) Oh bloody hell.
Margaret	What?
Pat	That bench. And the bus shelter. I can't believe it's just stayed like this all this time. (*She shakes her head to clear the memory.*) It's still dusty. It was always so dusty, and crisp bags blowing about —

They turn the corner into their old street. They stare at the boarded-up house. Pat looks up at the bathroom windows. She hears:

Voice of Vera I'm wetting my bloody pants here!

Voice of young Pat Oh, sorry, I didn't think you wore any!

Pat	You shove it all away, move on, grow up, cut your hair, and it's all there waiting, isn't it, waiting to be dealt with.
Margaret	I don't really know what you mean.
Pat	Look — go and get a taxi, find Bella — at least put that bit of it right. I'll get the cash biked over to you as soon as I can.
Margaret	Biked?
Pat	You go. This is my stuff. We've all got our nasty old wardrobes, haven't we? Where is she? She couldn't have got away, people don't.
Margaret	You did.
Pat	Everybody knows me. Why has she never tried to find me?
Margaret	She can't have wanted to. She can't have wanted to find either of us. (*She hears:*)

Voice of Vera I don't know what you're howling for — you never got on with her when she was here. Now go and post that bloody pools coupon.

Voice of young Margaret I did! I did get on with her! She'll come back for me anyway, she wouldn't leave me here with you.

Voice of Vera Are you cheeking me?

The next-door busybody looms up behind them.

68

Busybody   Do you recognise me? Next door! We always said you'd go far. *Lakeland Vet —* we loved that.

Another street on the same estate. Pat and Margaret walk along, checking the numbers.

Margaret   I just don't remember this family at all.
Pat   Well the mother was just like our mother, only vertical, but the daughter was really glamorous, had a little black shiny mac, really belted in, really high heels — big beehive, I used to hang over the gate, I just wanted to be her. Lorraine!
Margaret   This is it.

Jim's house. Claire and Mum are having yet more cups of tea.

Claire   Are you sure this is all right, waiting here for the bags? I thought it was safer.
Mum   No, that's fine. (*Lowering her voice.*) Anyway, I like Jim to be exposed to different types of women. Margaret's all very well in her way, but she's not upwardly mobile. I have a lovely friend who would take him on pronto, she's very high up in gum hygiene. A bit of a depressive but as I say to Jim, you don't want to be enjoying yourself all the time.
Claire   Ooh.
Mum   Kicking? Jim was the same, I had his foot in my kidneys from the July. In the event, he was all placenta and he had to wear a golliwog's jumper. He did. We

69

pulled him through but
that was it for me. I said
to my husband, twin beds
and a budgie.

*The closed gates of a large
modern house. Stella stands
with Billy and speaks into the
entryphone.*

Stella Mrs McIntyre? Could you let me in, please? My name's Stella Kincaid, you may have read my column, and I've got five thousand pounds in cash in my handbag.

A small and very untidy living-room. Lorraine, an unhappy-looking woman of about fifty, comes into the room where Pat and Margaret are waiting in company with three silent adolescents sprawled about. The room is dirty and cluttered.

Lorraine My mum says the last she heard Vera was cleaning at the Red Lion in town.
Pat Thanks.
Margaret We tried there. It's all new people now.
Lorraine Done well for yourself.
Pat Well, you know, right place at the right time.
Lorraine Is that it? Must have been in wrong place, me.
Pat Was it your sister who used to come past our gate on the way to work? Lorraine?
Lorraine That were me. Did you not recognise me?
Old mother (*from upstairs*) Lorraine! Hitch me up!
Lorraine (*to her mother*) Hang on! (*To Pat and Margaret.*) See yourselves out. You look older off, did you know?

The reception desk of the Kirkby Arms. Pat and Margaret are at the desk, trying to check in. Trainee receptionist Emma-Louise, nineteen, is on the computer. There is a 'do' on and drunk women in pink cocktail dresses are weaving in and out of the Ladies.

Pat   Let's start again. Has a Claire Wellesley checked in or left a message?
Emma-Louise   No.
Pat   Right. I would like a suite for me and a single for Miss Wellesley.
Emma-Louise   We don't have suites.
Margaret   They're bad for your teeth.

Emma-Louise	I can do you a large non-smoking ladies' with operational balcony.
Pat	Ladies'?
Emma-Louise	It's pink with cotton-wool balls and scatter cushions.
Pat	Whatever.
Emma-Louise	Could I trouble you for two forms of ID?
Pat	My face is my ID.
Emma-Louise	I'm afraid we don't accept faces.
Pat	My cards are coming with Miss Wellesley.
Emma-Louise	I'm fully comprehensive re that, it's just that with you having no cash or no credit cards, and given that we in the leisure industry have had our fingers fairly badly burned on this one.
Pat	I am Patricia Bedford.
Emma-Louise	Yes, but notwithstanding, I do have to adhere to the procedure. This is laid down, that we adhere to the procedure.
Pat	Fetch the manager.

Emma-Louise escapes behind the two-way mirror.

I don't believe this! ID! We were both plastered all over the Sunday papers this morning.

Two middle-aged ladies weave past.

First lady	I know how you feel, love.
Second lady	Look — it's her from *Glamor* — Valerie —
First lady	Valerie Lady Charleson. You were in a right quandary last week, weren't you?
Second lady	Give up on the publishing —
First lady	She didn't know whether to expand on the publishing side —
Second lady	Or give it all up.
First lady	Give it all up.
Second lady	Because Brent loves her.
First lady	He does, he does love you.

Mr Scruton, the seventeen-year-old hotel manager, stands behind the desk.

Second lady	Yeah, but he's never told her — he's only told Malcolm Halliday in the locker-room.
First lady	That's why she can't decide. (*In Valerie's voice.*) 'Don't hassle me, Brent! *Glamor* magazine needs me, and right at this moment in time — I just — don't — know!'

The two women burst into the Glamor *theme tune and stroll off back to their 'do', arms linked.*

Pat	You see? I don't need cash, I don't need ID. Those are my ID – the great marvellous warm caring British public!
Mr Scruton	As Emma-Louise may have mentioned, we do have to adhere to a procedure.
Pat	I don't care if you have to adhere to a baboon's bumhole. In fact compared with this rancid pile of olde-worlde knick-knacks a primate's backside begins to look like the epitome of gracious living.
Margaret	Could we not wait till our friend arrives with Pat's handbag?
Mr Scruton	While I have no objection to you sitting in the public areas, madam, I'm afraid your companion fails to meet the requirements of our dress code.
Pat	What?

Mr Scruton points to a printed card on the desk: MANAGEMENT REGRETS NO HEAVY WORK CLOTHES NO DENIMS NO SHELL SUITS. *As Pat stares at the notice, Stella and Billy in a cosy corner crack open the champagne.*

Pat's car heads towards a modern estate.

| Margaret | She's got this guest room and a shower, and those curtains, what are they, whooshed, ruched! She did say, any time . . . |

Bella's house. She opens the door and stares at Margaret and Pat.

Margaret	Bella. Did you read the papers this morning?
Bella	Yes I did. We all did. Very interesting to hear you've no friends and the job's rubbish. So I didn't bother putting you on next week's roster.
Margaret	The thing is, they make it up, virtually.
Bella	Do they, virtually? So you're not her sister and you're not off to Cali-Bloody-Fornia.

Margaret	I didn't say it. I came round to tell you that, and to just say is there any way Pat could have a bed for the night?
Bella	Not interested, sorry. I pity you, frankly, I had you down as genuine. I organised that coach trip, I made sure you were on that coach — you couldn't even be fagged to find me to come and say bye-bye.
Pat	Look — hang on —
Bella	Could you take your hand off my paintwork please. I'm not impressed with celebrities actually. From what I read they're thinking of taking off that *Glamor* anyway — so you'll be just another ex-has-been. Frankly I'm amazed your bosses let you dress like that. I don't know what you paid for that in LA, but round here they're going for ten ninety-nine.

She shuts the door. They turn away.

Pat	Bloody cheek. It was twelve quid.

Jim's house. Claire, on her ninth cup of tea, is flagging rather in the gloomy company of Mum.

Mum	Fibroids? Like baked potatoes.

Jim comes in cheerfully.

Jim	He's got all the bags no problem. So whenever you're ready he'll take you round to the hotel.
Claire	Oh that's marvellous. I'll just nip to the loo, then you must let me reimburse you for the tea.
Jim	Not to worry.
Mum	Don't stop her. With her bladder, this has cost me three pounds in Harpic alone.
Jim	I'll see she gets to the hotel all right, shall I?
Mum	Is that Margaret going to be there? Is that the scheme? Well I would think on hard and sharp before I got more convoluted with her, bluntly. She's playing you for a giddy kipper; she'll be laughing about you now with that sister.
Jim	If she's there I want to talk to her.
Mum	Well the chain goes on at the usual time.

Pat's car pulls up outside a corner shop. Margaret gets out and unlocks a small side door.

Margaret's bedsit. Margaret unlocks the door and goes straight to the cooker and lights all four jets. She's joined by Pat, who looks round the small room, furnished with nasty old pieces but brightened up with Margaret's ornaments and mug-trees, framed tea towels, etc.

Margaret   (*lighting the fire*) It'll warm up in a minute. (*She brings in a pint of milk from the window-sill and sniffs it.*)

Pat   Don't you have a fridge?

Margaret   There is a fridge but I wouldn't leave anything in it. It's off, sorry. Got some powdered.

Pat   What I could really do with is some food.

Margaret   I don't think I've got much in. Jim usually takes me Saturday, do a big shop. Well, he did.

Pat   That's OK. Look — shall I cook you my absolute favourite thing? It's really simple — you just need virgin olive oil, any pasta, beef tomatoes, fresh basil we can manage without — dried herbs then, and an avocado.

Margaret opens the door of her food cupboard and takes out, one by one, a 'Variety'-size packet of Special K, a small tin of spaghetti, a tin of powdered milk and a jar of pickle.

Margaret	That's what I've got. Does that count as pasta — tinned spaghetti? I don't have the things you have. I don't have three houses and a swimming-pool and an open-top —
Pat	Mercedes.
Margaret	This is me. This is where I live, and it's not nice — and I know I spent all yesterday saying I wasn't jealous and I was just glad to see you and I was happy living the way I do — well I'm not. I don't want to be like this — I want what you've got!
Pat	Then work for it! You've no idea what I had to do to get where I am now — do something!
Margaret	What can I do? I can't do anything. I wanted a husband and a house and a baby, well I told you what — you could do something — I couldn't do anything. I'm not clever, I couldn't be a manageress. I don't know how to earn any more money — other people have husbands, I can't buy a house, I'd have loved a little house — not a room where they come in when you're not here and look in your things — you had something.
Pat	Yes I did —
Margaret	Yes, well you should have helped me!
Pat	What?
Margaret	Why did you leave me?

There's a thumping on the wall. They look at each other.

Pat	That isn't what happened.
Margaret	It is what happened. You went. I was eleven. She got done again.
Pat	Suspended sentence.
Margaret	No — the real thing. It wasn't for long but — she never really got it together after that — I was just sort of fostered about. It wasn't that bad. I just used to think you might turn up. You know, sports car, trouser suit, just kid rubbish.

The doorbell rings.

My bell never rings.

She leaves the room. Pat looks around. On the bed is an extremely well-worn cuddly lion nightdress case, all bald. Pat touches it.

*Margaret opens the street door, to see Jim on the doorstep with Pat's handbag. The
limo is parked nearby.*

Margaret	Where did you get this?
Jim	Well, it's from Claire. Could you give it to Pat?
Margaret	How do you know Pat, I mean Claire?
Jim	I gave her a lift from London. I'd gone to see you, only you'd already come here.
Margaret	Well hello.
Jim	Hello.
Margaret	I did phone, loads of times.

They go to kiss.

	That bloody cardigan.
Jim	This? What's up with it?
Margaret	Oh nothing. I'm just sick of seeing it. Typical this isn't it. Missed you like mad since Friday, done a million exciting things, just wanted to come back and see you, and now —
Jim	What, you're wishing you hadn't?
Margaret	Oh I don't know. It's not as if Pat was happy either, and she's got everything. It was just nice to feel something was happening. You and me, nothing's happening.
Jim	I'm not with you.

Margaret	It's been a funny day, that's all. Look – come in and meet Pat – I feel like I've been wrong-footed all weekend 'cos she doesn't know anything about me and what I've got. I'm just feeling funny tonight – come in for a bit, eh?
Jim	Well, it's just that –
Margaret	What?
Jim	Well, Mum'll be putting the chain on quite soon.
Margaret	Phone her! Shove the door in! How long can we piddle along like this – she can't open her sardines, she can't unscrew her hot-water bottle – I want something. I want you to come in and meet my sister – my family – I've never asked you for anything – money, a baby – we should be able to ask each other for things – I want us to be together, but I can't always be accommodating everybody. Jim!
Jim	I'll go and phone Auntie Ivy –

Margaret Oh I'm tired of this. I knew she chose your underpants and took the peel out of your marmalade, but – I've had enough. That's us done – she's done it – I give in.

She slams the door on a puzzled Jim.

Margaret's bedsit. Pat gives Margaret a mug of tea.

Margaret Ta. Claire's at the hotel. That was Jim with your handbag for some reason, and we've just had a row and I've finished with him. You found the powdered milk then.

78

The bar of the Kirkby Arms. Jim is glooming over a drink with Claire.

Jim   You see, she's only thinking of me, my mother.

Claire   No that's not true.

Jim   Eh?

Claire   No, she's thinking of herself, which is fine and jolly sensible, as long as you do too. (*She stands up.*) What have I had? One orange juice — mad!

Claire goes off to the loo and Stella sees her go.

Stella   Pat's not going to track down the old mum is she? I mean we had a real stroke of luck there, we were way off beam. No, we have to get Pat to Vera's.

Billy   Well, that's going to be the photo, isn't it?

Stella scribbles on a piece of paper and waves at Jim.

Stella   Jim! Could you see Pat gets this?

Jim   Pardon?

Stella   Just a note from a fan, no need to mention me. Night night.

Margaret's bedsit.

Margaret   Pat?

Pat   Mm?

Margaret   Why didn't you take me with you? I were right tall, I could have passed for fourteen.

Pat   Did she say I'd run away? She chucked me out. I was pregnant.

Margaret   Did you have it?

Pat   Yes I did. It took bloody hours. No painkillers, just those awful women coming in and saying 'It'll get worse before it gets better, Pat Mottershead!' Never again.

Margaret   They have epidurals now.

Pat   They have stairlifts but I don't want one of them either.

Margaret   You could have come back after.

Pat   I did. Hobbled back straight after — all soggy bra and sanitary towels — no one there. She was inside I suppose. You and me couldn't have lived together. Ten and fifteen? There was a girl at the home — we hitched down to London, she knew a photographer, I did a bit of modelling. They laugh at Swinging London now but it was heaven on earth to me.

Margaret   Whose was it? The baby.

Pat   Do you remember my Saturday job in that café? The Swiss Cottage? Run by the only homosexual in north-east Lancashire? It was the boy who delivered the Pepsis I got pregnant with. We only did it once. He had a condom but he couldn't get it on. He thought that bit at the end had to go on as well. Come on, I'm buying you dinner.

Margaret   Where?

Pat   Mind your own business, Margaret Mottershead. Turn the fire off then, gas isn't cheap you know.

A dark side-street, full of closed businesses. Pat is leading Margaret towards the one lighted window — the Swiss Cottage Café. They go in.

The décor is a mixture of fifties coffee bar, all-night truck stop and 'Swiss' tea-shop. The customers are a strange mixture of obviously gay couples, deaf couples, art students and a few hard-faced blokes. Behind the counter is Pete, elegant, sixtyish, blue rinse and a cravat — the old-style queen. Pat approaches the counter.

Pete   Don't tell me. A bacon sandwich, a doughnut and a Pepsi float.

Pat   (*in original accent*) I'll pay you back Saturday.

They laugh and hug each other.

Pete   What can I get you?

Pat   A thirty-two.

Pete   With the double fried bread?

Pat   Of course. Margaret, phone Claire, she shouldn't miss out on this.

Margaret   You phone her, I'm choosing.

Pat   Cheeky.

The Swiss Cottage, a little later. Claire, Margaret and Pat are all very jolly over a bottle of wine. Pete brings over the plates.

Pete   There's your thirty-two, Patricia. Egg, chips and peas, Margaret.

Pat   That's Claire's — our Margaret doesn't like peas.

Claire   Yummee! This is such a treat, everybody. Chin chin.

Pat   None of it looks any different. You don't look any different.

Pete   I'm sixty-seven.

Pat   You're never.

Pete   Selling up. Soon as I can find a buyer. Quit while you can still smack the ketchup, that's my feeling.

Margaret It's lovely. I'm very impressed with these chips.

Pat   Margaret's in chips. Pete — you don't know where my mother ended up, do you? Our mother.

Pete   The terrible Vera. Well we used to see her hanging round the Red Lion, but that's twenty years ago.

Pat   We've asked at the Red Lion.

Pete   Now, who would know?

Claire   Aargh!

Pete   Oh my God, boiling water somebody!

Claire   The note!

Pat reads Stella's note.

The gates of the modern house, as before. The next morning.

Pat	This can't be right.
Margaret	The note only said she'd be here this morning, it didn't say she lived here. She might be the cleaner.
Pat	She might run a mobile blow-job service. (*Pause.*) I don't want to see her.
Margaret	You've got to.
Pat	This is making me sick.
Margaret	She'll just be a little old lady. Come on, let's get it over with. It's this one.

They walk into the house. Odd pieces of furniture are on the lawn and piled up in the hall. Pat and Margaret go up the stairs and stop in the bedroom doorway. The room is in chaos, clothes and shoes everywhere. There is a noise from the bathroom. Pat and Margaret move over to the doorway. A figure with its back to them is packing toiletries into a supermarket trolley bag. She turns and stares at them with no expression, then carries on packing.

Vera	Bit late for Mother's Day, aren't you?
Pat	Actually, we were hoping to visit your grave but we're a bit early.

Vera	I suppose it were too good to last, you had to track me down eventually. You want to get your neck done — Pat — you can be in and out in two days.
Pat	Recognise Margaret?
Vera	Can't miss her. What do you do?
Margaret	I work on the motorway — in the cafeteria.
Vera	Your father wasn't much cop at anything either. (*She goes into the bedroom and starts holding clothes up against herself.*)
Pat	Have the press been here?
Vera	About the villas? They're in my name but I've never seen a penny.
Pat	No — what have you been saying about me?
Vera	Nothing. I don't know anything about you. I know you're on the telly, but we only watch the dog trials. Tricky colour, lime green.

Pat and Margaret sit down on the bed.

Pat	I didn't realise prostitution was so lucrative.

Vera	I don't think it is. I think you have to enjoy it to earn big money. I didn't mind the sex but I was never very good at talking to them.
Pat	So where did all this come from?
Vera	Pools.
Pat	Not the bloody pools!

The atmosphere starts to loosen. Vera looks through her dressing-table drawers.

Vera	That was the start. Won the bloody pools. Ticked no publicity, Caribbean cruise, met my Robert — he couldn't believe it — own teeth, a few bob and I could do shorthand.
Pat	Lovely.

Vera   (*moving out on to the landing*) He's skipped off now, of course. Rat. What do you want, I'm busy. If your paw's out wanting money, forget it, it's tied up and you're way down the queue.

The removal men pass her and go into another bedroom.

Pat   You've got a nerve.

Vera   Have I? You're here to tell me she doesn't want a few bob?

Pat   Why shouldn't she? This is your child, this is the little girl you left at eleven because you couldn't be fagged looking after her. She's not going to get what she wanted then — love, care — a mother — we're thirty years too late with that one — money's all you've got isn't it, and she hasn't got any — yes I should think she does want a few bob.

Vera   Don't call *me*. No one barred you from tracking her down. You earn a decent living, I've seen you in the paper meeting Prince frigging Philip – you could have helped her yourself, but you're like me.

Pat   That's right. I'm like you. I never had a father. I'm assuming her father wasn't my father. I only had you – brought up the Vera way, what could I know – housework stinks and black bras don't show the dirt. What else – don't be warm, don't be kind, look after number one, stuff any other bugger who does different – you made me, you stupid cow, and you ballsed up.

Vera   Did I? Did I? Would you have got out if I hadn't shoved you out? You want to be warm, you want to be kind, fine – you end up slopping gravy about for eighty quid a week. You should be thanking me for making you hard inside, because that's what's pushed you on, that's what's kept you going – there's a million bloody actresses out there, aren't there? Paying her? You should be paying me.

Margaret   I don't want anything.

The removal men pass them and go down the stairs with a china panther each.

Vera   'Course you do. But we don't all get what we want. I did my share, two kids in a rotten council house, nosy neighbours, useless bloody husband smoking himself to death. What does it all matter now? We're just three middle-aged women getting through this sod of a life.

There's a flash of a camera, and the three women are caught by Stella and Billy at the bottom of the stairs.

Stella Oh that will be a nice one. Vera, could we have you with the panthers?
Vera You can have me in a hammock with an Instant Whip, you're paying. Would you excuse me, I must have a word with the bailiffs.

Vera leaves. Pat realises she's been done over and the fight goes out of her. It takes Margaret longer to catch up. They sit down on a set of fancy dining-chairs outside the front door.

Pat	The note from the fan.
Stella	But I'm a huge fan, darling.
Pat	How much have you paid her?
Stella	Only five. Not enough to leave the country which is what she really wants. You wouldn't believe how many lives she's ruined.
Pat	Wouldn't we?

Pat and Margaret exchange a smile.

Stella	So your jigsaw's shaping up very nicely, Pat. Vera's jail sentence, your nude modelling.
Pat	Oh come on, that was a fashion shot.
Stella	And of course your baby. (*Pause.*) It's very easy to trace an adoption these days you know.
Pat	Oh I know. He traced me. He's a trainee physiotherapist in Winnipeg. That's not such a good headline for you, is it? 'Pat Bedford's secret baby is a Canadian.'
Stella	No, they're very bad news, the old Canadians.
Pat	Still, you've got plenty to send me down the tubes without him.
Margaret	(*standing up as her chair is removed by one of the men*) This is really unfair, this. What's Pat ever done? Had a father who died, had a mother who didn't know the meaning of the word. 'Cos really, Mum, she were crap. Sorry — but — she had a baby at fifteen, that's an accident, there's no shame, and he's fine — physiotherapy thingy — then she only goes on to become one of the biggest actresses on American television — what has she done wrong? You haven't, have you our Pat?

Pat   You tell the network. They're the ones who'll panic. How many *Peyton Place*s did Mia Farrow do after she ran off with Frank Sinatra? She's had to adopt twelve Vietnamese orphans just to earn a living.

Margaret (*to Stella*) Well I don't know how you can live with yourself.
Stella   I don't produce the dog poo darling, I just try to stop people planting geraniums in it. Though you're right in a way Margaret, it is a marvellous story. Wouldn't take too much to make you almost sympathetic, Pat.
Pat   And you'd do that, would you Stella?
Stella   Well I might. You tell me everything, Margaret tells me everything.
Margaret Me?
Stella   We've got it all then, you see. This is Roseanne Barr with knobs on.

Pat still hasn't caught on.

Margaret	Opray Winfrey. Janet Jackson.
Pat	God I'm thick.
Stella	We've got abuse, neglect, prostitution, missing sisters, lost babies, rags to riches. We're talking twelve weeks at number one here, film rights, mini-series . . .
Pat	Who'd play Margaret?
Margaret	Meryl Streep.
Pat	What about Vera though?
Stella	We'd have to tie her down to an exclusive. Otherwise she's a bit of a loose hypodermic.

Vera strolls over to join them.

Vera	Sorry to be so long. I was defrosting some kidneys.
Pat	Anyone we know?
Margaret	Mum — did you ever love us?

Vera	I don't think so. I don't think I knew what love was till I bred my first Afghan.
Stella	You see, what we really need is a happy ending.
Vera	Funnily enough, that's just what I was going to talk to my daughter about.

Pat and Margaret look at each other, unsure which daughter she means.

The kitchens of the Kirkby Preston Services, later that day. Pat is giving away signed photographs and being very charming. Margaret approaches Bella tentatively.

Margaret	I never said the job was rubbish. I love the job.
Bella	Look − I am up to here in the wrong − I am just one big arsehole at times − everything in the papers were wrong − job's here if you want it.
Margaret	I don't know. Can I take a week of my holidays − sort myself out?
Spotty boy	(*panicking behind the counter*) Bella − we're out of chips.
Bella	Keep your acne on, terminator. Have a fabulous week, you deserve it.
Margaret	Jim's not around is he?
Bella	Not turned up. That Syreeta's hopping mad 'cos she's had to mop the urinals.

Margaret waves her arm and leaves.

Outside Jim's house, the same afternoon. A miserable Jim is removing the name-strip from inside his windscreen, while Mum dusts the front gate. Pat's limo pulls up and Margaret gets out.

Margaret　Jim? Do you want to make it up or not?

Mum　Now, just a minute —

Margaret　No conferring. If we're doing it, then we have to get a place, live together, none of this fannying about. We either go for it or it's finito.

Mum　There'll be no living together if I have anything to do with it.

Jim　You don't have anything to do with it, so button up or ship out — it's your fault they never learned me to read and I could never get a qualification. Yes — you're on, Margaret — I've loved you from the first minute you gave me extra gravy — you've given me care and comfort and a wonderful sex life. Come here.

They embrace.

Mum	A sex life? You've had a sex life? Where have you had it?

Jim stops kissing Margaret long enough to answer.

Jim	On your bed.
Mum	Not on the eiderdown.

Heathrow Airport, a few days later. Pat's car is parked, and she is directing operations as a sweating porter loads her baggage on to a trolley, watched by Claire and Margaret. Pat is on a mobile phone.

Pat	I beg your pardon? You can't promise to deliver them by Friday? In that case I can't promise to wear them for the Oscars, pose in them for *Vogue* magazine, or indeed patronise your tacky little third-rate operation on any future occasion. Good morning.
Porter	Bloody hell.
Pat	Yes, that's the heavy one. Claire, you check the bags in, I'll meet you in the VIP lounge, with . . .
Claire	Right you are.

Pat	I can't believe I'm doing this.
Claire	Well, I think it's a brilliant wheeze, jolly well done you.
Pat	I wish Margaret would change her mind.
Claire	Would make the whole thing jollier, wouldn't it?
Pat	Oh, here.

She hands over a bag with a baby's cardigan in it. Claire hugs her, remembers to give her her handbag.

Claire	Safe journey.
Pat	You too. Come on.

She hustles Margaret through the doors.

You could still come, you know — I book an extra seat for the make-up.

Margaret laughs.

Margaret	I know there's nowt doing here, but what can we do, we have to give it a go.
Pat	I just quite fancied spending some time with somebody who didn't think the sun shone out of my backside.
Margaret	Oh no, so it doesn't.
Pat	Well I'll need you to visit.
Margaret	You blooming well will.
Pat	Bye.

They manage a clumsy hug.

Hang on. (*She pulls out a set of keys and an envelope from her bag.*)

Margaret	What are them?
Pat	It says in the letter — I'll see you.

She hurries off. Heads turn and look at her. A woman near Margaret stares at Pat.

Woman   That's her off *Dynasty* — Stephanie Beacham.

Margaret   Shut your mouth till you're less ignorant. (*She marches off, very pleased with herself.*)

The VIP lounge, a little later. Pat is trying to relax with a magazine. A stewardess bends over her. A woman next to her is reading a newspaper.

Stewardess   Champagne, Miss Bedford? Mrs . . . ?

Vera puts down her paper and takes a drink.

Vera   Just call me Vera. Cheers! (*She looks over at Pat's magazine.*) Who's that then?

Pat   That's Jackie Stallone, Sylvester's mother. And that's Liz Taylor's mother. They're very big at the moment, celebrities' moms.

Vera   Oh, are they?

Pat winces as she realises what she's said.

The Swiss Cottage Café, a few nights later. Through the window we can see the café is closed and the chairs are on the tables. Jim is mopping the floor and Margaret happily polishes the red neon 'Café' sign. The camera swoops away from their little lighted haven into the night sky as we . . .

. . . fade to black.

Pat and Margaret was first shown on BBC TV in September 1994 with the following cast:

Margaret   Victoria Wood
Pat   Julie Walters
Claire   Celia Imrie
Billy   Don Henderson
Stella   Deborah Grant
Jim   Duncan Preston
Bella   Lynda Rooke
Sue   Jan Alphonse
Daisy   Amanda Pointer
Jim's mother   Thora Hird
Maeve   Anne Reid
Helper in old age home   Julie Hesmondhalgh
Old lady in home   Gabrielle Blunt
Martin, warm-up man   Philip Lowrie
Porter   Charles Pemberton
Vera, in home   Joane Hall
Vera   Shirley Stelfox

Pete   Robert Kingswell
Nadia   Sue Wallace
Busybody   Frances Cox
Mr Scruton   Adam Warner
Hotel Manager   Roger Brierley
Emma-Louise   Gemma Wardle
First lady in motel   Madge Hindle
Second lady in motel   Angela Curran
Mr Lloyd   Tenniel Evans
Spotty boy   Corrin Helliwell
Stringer   Peter Lorenzelli
First fan   Helen Lindsay
Second fan   Vera Jakob
Tea bar lady   Jeillo Edwards
Margaret, aged two   Melissa Allen
Pat, aged seven   Sammy-Jo Smith

Producer   Ruth Caleb
Director   Gavin Millar
Casting Advisor   Susie Bruffin
Script Editor   Robyn Slovo
Music composed by   Colin Towns
Associate Producer   Matthew Hamilton
Film Editor   Ken Pearce
Production Designer   Ken Starkey
Photography   John Daly
First Assistant Director   Daphne Phipps
Location Manager   Adam Richards
Continuity   Cecilia Coleshaw
Production Co-Ordinator   Lucy Ainsworth-
Taylor
Finance Assistant   Tanya Latif
Assistant Directors   Beni Turkson
Dave Reid
Regina Dunphy

Art Director   Nic Pallace
Property Buyer   Katie Spencer
Construction Manager   Peter Toller
Camera Assistants   Steve Wallace
Steve Banks
Grip   Tex Childs
Sound Recordist   Malcolm Campbell
Boom Operator   Richard Jupp
Gaffer   Terry Montague
Make-up Designer   Christina Baker
Make-up Assistant   Debbie Taylor
Costume Designer   Anna Stubley
Costume Assistant   Nadia Nigoumi
Assistant Film Editor   Louise Leonard
Graphics Designer   Rosie Turner